Late Arrival

Late Arrival

Poems by

Susan Dines

Cover design by Shay Culligan
Cover image by Jordi Moncasi on Unsplash
Author photo by Kaela Speicher Photography

ISBN: 978-1-63980-848-9

Kelsay Books
502 South 1040 East, A-119
American Fork, Utah 84003
Kelsaybooks.com

For my mother, Evelyn Stewart Stevens:

Your absence has gone through me
Like thread through a needle.
Everything I do is stitched with its color.

—W.S. Merwin

Acknowledgments

The author would like to thank the editors of the following journals, wherein these poems first appeared:

American Writers Review: “The Fugitive’s Wife When Expecting the Feds”

The Comstock Review: “The Guestbook at Winchester Lookout”

Kestrel, A Journal of Literature and Art: “King Street”

North Dakota Quarterly: “Ache and Awe,” “Dropping in”

Smoky Blue Literary and Arts Magazine: “The Cracker Jack Prize”

A special thanks to the University of Iowa, Tucson Festival of Books, and Fish Publishing for recognizing the following poems:

“Best Wishes to the Next Bride”—shortlisted for the 2021 Fish Poetry Prize

“Blame It on Maine”—winner of the University of Iowa Hawkeye Haiku Contest

“Sea Glass”—placed third in the 2021 Tucson Festival of Books Writing Competition

I would like to express my deepest gratitude to my family for their unwavering support throughout this journey. To my husband, for encouraging me to go after my dreams—however delayed they may have been. To my daughters, Brook Bluebaugh and Shelby Burns, for living authentic and adventurous lives that inspire me daily.

A special thanks to Karen Kelsay for choosing this book. The editorial team and cover artist at Kelsay Books deserve recognition for their guidance, support, and creativity.

Heartfelt thanks to my friend and second reader, Arlene DeMaris, my go-to person for feedback and encouragement. I am also appreciative of April Bernard, Gregory Pardlo, Craig Morgan Teicher, and Carmen Giménez, each of whom have read many of the poems included in this book and provided generous guidance that helped shape my work.

For their friendship and continued support, I am grateful for all the members of my writing groups. Sending a special shout out to poet and spoken word artist John Burroughs; thank you for remembering the poetry slam, my Doc Martens, and being so kind as to share your thoughts on my work.

Finally, my sincere gratitude to poet and punk rocker Gerry LaFemina, who opened the door to a "fairer house" for my words to reside.

Contents

4. Arrival

1. First Flight

It’s true. I’ve been delayed more than Jet Blue, but who’s counting
the hours of my human misconstruings, my racking up flyer miles
while going nowhere, this body hitched to another’s journey,
another’s maneuvers—
another’s spine.

Ache & Awe

It’s the
awe that
sucks you in,
lulls your senses
goodbye, dulls
your gut instinct
until intuition is a
web of white tulle
laid out before the
altar. Now, how easily
you’ll fall for the puff-
ery of matrimony, all
those fattened stars
steadfast in their flick-
ery, little distractors
from the sickle moon
with its treacherous
edges. See how the
crescent cuts the trust-
ing sky like a sharpen-
ed tongue to come
from the once tender
lips that tripped all your
switches, red flags slip-
ping to half-mast—
mask slipping like wis-
dom & wit, & later, the
ache when you realize
it’s not just the moon
that has its phases—
it’s not just the
moon that
wanes

The Favorite Line

> *Linda would have liked her own husband,*
> *whose intelligence had once impressed her,*
> *to simply disappear.*
> —Elizabeth Strout, *Anything Is Possible*

It's hard to ignore the favorite line of a book, how it strikes the bell of the familiar, spells out absolute truth—or something close to it, the thought you dare not admit to revisit on occasion (or more often than that), but now it's there, the black and the white of it, letters, the i's and the l's lined up like straight-edge razors—and

the others—the more curvaceous characters, so obvious as they
spectacle along the clotheslines of the page, exposed little
exhibitionists—those s's and o's—funny how a line can take you
by surprise, provoke an admission or a lie.

When Your Spouse Flees the Country

The FBI will scatter about
your house, black windbreakers

swishing through foyer and kitchen.
One man will enter the private space

of your mostly modest walk-in closet,
his sensible agent-approved shoes

clashing with your wild exhibit
of leopard-print flats, custom

Chucks, and thigh-high suede boots.
He will pause, then unpurse his lips

and begin to speak with all the personality
of a plain white tube sock: “You have a lot

of shoes.” He’ll say this as if the stash
were criminal contraband or the product

of ill-gotten gain. My mind will instantly
leap to Imelda Marcos—Zappos—

my husband's "supposed" white-collar
crime, and just as I consider these

minimum-security sins, I'll consider the time
and whether these curious men will still

be eyeing my things when the school bus
pulls up—and my two daughters bolt

through the house in their new neon yellow
Doc Marten boots.

The Fugitive's Wife When Expecting the Feds

My head

at 2:52 this morning, ignoring my hand's promise
to write down my alibi, transcribe every hindsight—
before the sun fingers the lineup of pines and files
through my kitchen blinds—before the heat, the tea-
pot, the whistle—before the bread turns to toast

it persists

with its worst-case scenarioing, its emergency
broadcasting, its firing of one battered synapse
that catapults me up and over the clueless dog
and onto the blurry blue sofa, where a lifted screen
strikes my eyes with light so bright, I type on keys
from memory, something so urgent it needs spilling—
before the sun, the tea, and the toast—before the hard
knock on my door, the flick of a wrist, the flash of a badge.

.

Wanted Person, US Marshals Headquarters, Arlington

When three agents stormed the gate
to my pool, I rushed to the water's edge
to recover my top—breaststroke—
only the backstroke could have held
their attention longer—long enough
to have allowed for my husband
to rocket over the fence—had he not
already rocketed over Canada's fence.
I don't know who was more shocked,
but I can guess the agents were not
that upset by my unrestrained breasts
and suspect talk of their brief surfacing
may have slipped into the conversation
of the camo-clad assembly of men later
that day as they filled up on consolatory
burgers and beers. And though I would
normally be humiliated by such indignities,
being they were in pursuit of something
much bigger, I've decided to chalk it all
up to a minor price to pay for what would
eventually lead to of the apprehension
of my soon-to-be ex. Indeed, these methods
by which to be freed from such a partner
may seem a bit extreme . . .

but who's to question karma, her means
and measures—she knows better than most
that some men don't leave as quietly as others—
some even need to have hands clicked into cuffs
and body hauled from the grounds.

Emptying My Husband's Pockets

It's just something I've learned
from peeling his wet, limp
bills from the drum of our washing
machine, usually a few singles or
a twenty, not a total loss—
not like the hundred and fifty
thousand he buried beneath the crooked
canopy of a sycamore. Had he any
affinity for trees, he would have known
this variety grows close to water.
I almost warned him of the danger.

Almost.

But my mouth sealed shut as he
concealed his treasure with such
authority—so I spoke
not a word. Many years after he hid
his cash and had fled the country, I led
the agents of the U.S. Department
of the Treasury to the money tree.

Turns out I was right about the water—
seems all the dollars lost to the laundry
taught me a thing or two. Yet, nothing
prepared me for their fists—
dripping greedy with the monetary
slop, their disbelief as it oozed through
their calculating fingers like rotten
avocados. And I couldn't help it, but
the corners of my mouth lifted a bit.

Still, I spoke not a word—of my glee—
my complete and utter delight. It was like
witnessing the carnage of my washer.

But better.

Duality

. . . the soul's bliss / and suffering are bound together
—Jane Kenyon

I can only guide my daughter's eyes to the Pacific—can't
separate the foil flicker of water from the surface chop.

And there's no awaiting the delicate drape
of ivory froth, skirting, lace-like, across the shoreline

without what came before it—the dangerous, thunderous
breaker. I can't isolate the one, leaving only the other—

can't yank the yin from the yang—
for it's this contradiction that elevates the worth,

the wonder, in the beholder. We come to treasure
the washed-up, sand-scratched, gauzy green sea

glass because we know of its antonym, the broken
sharp shard that once cut us.

2. Missed Connection

I guess I knew what the answer was all along—
it pushed back like a headwind or hovered
in the holding pattern—year upon
languorous year of holding
my tongue.

Remixed Sonnet: No Defense Against Eros and Other Fancies of Flight

A still life, not still, his will pulls at my pulse that keeps pace with his stride. / Here I am tabled like crumpet (or culprit), either way, prey to the Windhover's / hunger. I am captive (or captivated) by his relentless surveillance and his glorious glide. / But how can he honor his honor when his mission risks volta like lust risks lover. // By day, he's Tern turning up clues in what's brackish, by night Great Horned Owl / whose devotion is to tracking the skin with binocular vision. See how his eyes / decode this body—its lingo, as they make sharp their focus, premise, and prowl. / Their vision is tunnel and skillful, little heat-seeking missiles that don't try // to target more than what's instinct or premeasured in the royal blue promise of prize. / They stalk like government agent on suspect—his interest is suspect—suspended / like violet or lilac . . . or something like that—a shifting—like person of interest revised / interested, like turn and turn and—*watch, watch yourself—it's here where you amend—* // surrender—slip up and get plucked from the skirt of the shore! See how eyes pry, beckon / the hidden, violate, then invite—watch—watch them wink Washington, then Charleston.

In Bed with the Omniscient Narrator

he slides bolt—
lifts lock from latch
his heart picks up pace
someplace between
run! and in too deep
but when eyes meet
her pupils give secrets up
like snitch—or poet
like gate thrust
all the way   open
he listens like criminal
agent trapped between
code and libido
restraint waning
his hands slip
no—not slip—grip
both her wrists
detects uptick in pulse
swish—swish—swish
runs the analysis (can't help it)

can’t stop
the gravitational pull
the magnetism
the push up
against rock wall
where waves crest
and hips quicken
where power shifts
in the silver spark-shivers
in the sea foam
lap—lapping—firecracking
under the full and
unstoppable moon

3. Next Carrier

I would grow smaller as the carrier climbed higher,
looking down from my window
at where I once stood.

My Bridgerton Name

> *First, you'll start with Lord or Lady, followed by your middle name. From there, add the last thing you drank with "ton" at the end.*
>
> —Alexis Morillo, *Bustle*

according to TikTok is Lady

Lynn Ice Latteton of Meadowshire,

which, in keeping with custom,

automatically entitles me entrance

to the next lavish ball, where I will

feel the need to flee any man whose

name is written on the dance card

ribboned to my wrist. I'll slip out

the back and take a solo spin around

a proper English garden, losing myself
amongst the lilacs, wisteria, and
hollyhocks. Then, like a good spin
spoiled, I will become unexpectedly
and most regrettably engaged to Lord

Evan Red Bullton of Parkshire, who, too,

was caught wandering about the garden—

unaccompanied, he with his wandering

eye, and I, folded over the violets, spilling

over my corset—the town gossip as witness.

.

A Friend Recommends Charles Simic's *Walking the Black Cat*

Strangely enough, her supposed crime got exposed

in a most innocent of venues, disrupting the hush

of the local public library—but the look on his face—

you'd think she pulled another man's recklessness

from her purse, not his, the one who, on a whim,

wrangled the wedding ring onto her flinching finger

in that humid Charleston courtyard under last August's

reddening moon. *What's this about,* he questioned,

frantically waving the bar napkin she had possessed

only seconds ago, then flicking his wrist as if flashing

an official badge or a smoking gun. And she got it—

the panic, the probable cause, the confusion. After all,
there's the man's name in unfamiliar script to consider,
the air, now, cologned with the crisp, citric scent of muddled
lime and mint, the sweat from her mojito's glass commingled
with the black ink, evidencing something more torrid,
a blurred truth that left only the poet's name intact, while
Walking the Black Cat morphed into something more
suspicious like, *Walk Out Back.* Oh, Charles Simic, if only
you could witness this spectacle you caused between these
stacked shelves of our respectable Dewey Decimal system.

Ornamental

        I agreed

to power out-
side of myself.

A trimming
suspended

from crimson
ribbon.

        I dangled

the arm
of a con-

color fir
that smelled

of larceny
and lust.

I was not much

for this
entangled tin

that tinseled
the truth—nor

was I made
brighter from its

twisted lights
laid on thick.

I wasn't made more

by adorning
the vainglorious thing.

Serial Spouse

Sauve / qui peut—let those who can save themselves / save themselves

—Sharon Olds

I've had my share of husbands—
more than my share of reeling
around and around on another
and another of those run down
playground merry-go-rounds.
Here I go again, I'd say, as I
stepped up onto the platform,
the taste of rust alarming the top
of the tongue. And why would I
hope for anything other than what
was foggily disclosed through
my defective diamond decoder
ring: always the same slanted grin
before the shove of the handholds,
harder and harder, his black oxfords
planted firmly in the dirt as I spin.

I've tried   to time   my dismounts

in between the hands that send this
spiraling disk dizzying, but there's
no easy stopping the circling—
the momentum that holds the flesh
down against the repeated pattern.

On Divorcing Lord Evan Red Bullton

pull / up / anchor / or / jump / ship /
you / got / this / you / got / this
—Taurus (translated)

no hem of shore / to skirt / nor dream / of light / to harbor / no sextant / for sighting / Taurus, his charge / of darkness / flashes of luminous dots and dashes / bullish with code

.--. ..- .-.. .-.. / ..- .--. / .- -. -.-. .... --- .-. / --- .-. / .--- ..- -- .--. / ... .--. / -.-- --- ..- / --. --- - / - .... / -.-- --- ..- / --. --- - / - ....

I spot / his aerial plea / his celestial tweet / but with no decoder / I choke like dying / wind or dropped sail / I make two fists / and wait / for a rogue wave / to hit / this listing ship

Dick and Jane/Fun in Family Court

okay here it is   the truth   the whole truth
and nothing but   Jane woke up   on the edge
of a dream this morning   everything screamed
Fight   and she did   and guess what
the judge was in   her corner   told her she aims
too low   should ask   for more
but even with this   assurance
Jane spoke out   a low number   she knows not
to ask for more   than can be concealed
in a paper bag   and be slid   across
a sticky table   in the back corner
of a dark bar   she took less
there is no   justice   in politics
where truth   wanes   like   a sickle
moon   cuts you   into little   bits
Look, look.   See?
See Dick   See Dick run
his mouth   like funhouse
mirror   See Dick suck   up to judges
just   to abuse   his power
See Dick   take and take   pleasure
in the disparity   he stashes   in partisan
pockets   deep   with favors
to call in   when those smaller   call out
for justice   or just fall   and   fall
off the cliffs   of dreams   and question
should she have done   more   should she
have not settled   should she have stood
in the courtroom   over the trap door   once more

The Cracker Jack Prize

It's pretty much the point
of it all why we push past
the cornballs reach
blindly into the narrow
pocket of a box not
knowing what
we will come up with but
we press on the flesh
of our mortal fingers blocking
out the light
feeling around in the dark
for some sharp corner
we'll need
to dig deeper
to excavate the essential
marvel that can save us
from every heavy thing

Leaving My Lawyer's Office

After the glide
of my pen

across the final
fetter—

I am life-
boat, unmoored,

riding the rise
of each

welcomed swell.
My mind eases

to the speed of sail—
then buoy.

Light blazes down
like blessing
.

Best Wishes to the Next Bride

I stoop for the last time
and leave

his name under the doormat
for the next

bride to take. I'm not liable
for future takers: *Enter*

at your own risk
the marriage contract should state—

yes, of course, in italics.

Who really knows who truly lies
and lies beside you in bed,

head hidden
in the white fluff of pillow,

hand tucked
under the Egyptian

cotton sheet, fingering the
smooth line of the spine

of the knife—
just before slicing

best wishes to bits
and pieces.

Next time I’ll read
the wall, the hieroglyphics—

all the figures I saw—
but ignored.

Next time I’ll think
thrice before I jot

down my name— . . ..
sign on another damn dotted line.

Dropping In

My daughter, left foot
bracing
the back of her skateboard, hovers
over the edge, then commits
with her right foot to taunting
gravity. Now, nothing
but vertical

drop,
banked walls, and
concrete coaster ahead.
My marriages,
I think,
have a similar vibe—
that song, *Flirtin' with*
Disaster, too, how I sang

along with my Molly
Hatchet 8-track back when
I was her
age, the lyrics, my only
company as I sped down
the Jersey Turnpike, heading
to embrace
the next

treacherous weather system.
Why do we favor storm
chaser over shelter . . .
or is that just me? Why not

give helmets and
knee pads
as wedding gifts—why not
be honest?

My daughter rotates 180
degrees in the air, smacks
the center of her board on
the feature's lip,
then reenters
the bowl—this trick
is called a disaster.

4. Arrival

I know it’s late, but it wasn’t until I ignored
the seatbelt light, its safety in restraint, did I see
the time I had squandered, the sun setting
fire to the horizon. But do you see me now,
see my death grip on the joystick
as I make the final approach
to my late arrival?

The Guestbook at Winchester Lookout

Fresh off a breakup, I tell myself: *a change*
of scenery will refresh me. One mile in, I see
a man. With flowers. The pendulum of clichéd
daisies swung from his hand as he trudged toward
the lookout. He'd go missing in the switchbacks—

then resurface. I trailed behind in case the flowers
were for a beloved pacing at the summit,
awaiting on a proposal or some other romantic
undoing as the sun rolled her large round eye
below the opposing peaks. But before I got to
the top, he'd already begun his descent—hands
vacant, head slanted down, no fiancée in tow, his eyes
fixed low on the rough patch ahead, pocked with ruts
and washouts. Just as the stranger slid past, a sound
startled me—something . . .
being crushed, made smaller. I jerked to the right,
cut my arm on the sharp stubble of a huckleberry
shrub—then remembered the bright red tissue paper
that barely clung to the bouquet, fussed in the wind
so much, it was one good gust away from coming
completely undone. *Good*—I thought—*he carried*
the paper out of the park—not a litterer—probably
not a murderer either, then. I made it to the overlook
where a detached whip of cloud stood to admire itself
in the slate gray lake below. Beside me leaned a white
wooden structure. Inside, a well-wrecked guestbook
rested on a forest green bench. Next to it, those daisies.
The book's cover buckled a bit, and the corners

(one crushed, three missing) exposed lined pages within. I signed my name and then went on to explore the others, but I didn't make it past the entry above mine, which proceeded with, *In loving memory.* The three names of the departed, I can't recall. But I'll never forget *his* name, the man recording his misfortune, signing beneath:

Scott (Daddy)—in brackets, which got me thinking back to what Creeley said: *Strong feeling wants a container.*

At the Sanctuary Café

Dead to me—yes—but their ghosts are still hot
and humid and home, the two of them

wrestling with the broken air conditioning.
They're prolific with grunts and volleyed

stories of past athletic glories and politics
and influence and wins! and wins! and wins!

But it's not the lack of air or their lips manic
with mythomania that drove me here—it is this—

the toasted homespun muffin, thick with fresh-
carved country ham and free-range egg tucked

under a cover of white cheddar and cave-aged
gruyère, crisping thin and lacey on extended edges—

plated and readied for the sweet red-berry jelly
and house fiery mustard, set side by side

in two pleated cardboard cups, like two
catholic schoolgirls in pleated skirts (rolled up),

pledging allegiance to the sweet and the fiery.

Barnacle Billy's Webcam,
Wednesday, 8:16 AM

And for the first time, under my watch, one of the anchored boats, a fixed feature on my screen, lurches forward, its smoke startling an idle sky. Two figures scramble about the stern (I think that is the correct term for the back of a boat) like they are readying for work, but instead of holding to-go bagels between clenched teeth while wrestling silk ties into proper Windsor knots, they wrestle with rope of heavy hemp, unknot rusted lobster traps from a cluster of cerulean and yellow striped buoys. As the cluttered boat slips under

the wooden drawbridge, it deposits a white brush stroke
of a wake that ruffles the still life of the cove. And for some
reason I'm annoyed. Still, I continue to watch the vessel
head toward the gritty gray horizon, carting off the men
all set to mark their territory, stake their liquidous land.

Erasure at St. Cecelia's Grade School After My Mother's Death

Mrs. Desmond welcomes me back
to no place I've ever been. Her softened tone
confirms she knows of my loss. I take my seat
and fixate on the gray metal tray at the base
of the chalkboard, the eraser parked there
like a miniature black hearse. No other sixth grader
dares to glance my way—hair still fragrant with
frankincense. I am the girl who is eclipsed
by the church that sits in the belly of this school,
erased by the priest who pendulumed the incense my way.

And here in my homeroom, sitting at my desk, I know
it's supposed to be me, but how easy it is to go from a *me*
to a *she*—she's the broken one—see her turn
toward the window and watch the tufted buttons
of clouds line the lid of the sky, nod to their dark
undersides, make a pact to never love another—risk
the cliff of their illness, let the slick leather soles of her
saddle shoes lose their grip. And when it's time for Choir,
time to stand shoulder to shoulder with the others
in the loft of the very church that made official
her mother's departing, she will begin to sing, lips
quivering—then close her mouth tight like a casket.

Errors in Eros

She should have   known
she'd get it   wrong
an adult   still   subtracting
on her fingers   all the missing
If it's not one thing   it's your mother
the experts assure   as they pore over
the unmeasurable   with their box
plots   stem diagrams   and pie
charts   but who can   truly
assess   death's effect
on   a child's ability   to invite
healthy relationships   later in life
The poets point   to November's
fractured   light
the low-slung   cloud-
ing   of the earth—   tied child
Is she   not liable
for   her   words
etched in ether's   amethyst
ash   her   clenched fists
her   hell-
bent stance   on that   black-
top lot   behind the giftshop
pact spoken   & spun
like spilled ladder   like unlatched salt
like black mirror   like cracked cat

Inheritance

The weatherman predicts high winds,
                a steady slant of air advancing

at menacing speeds. A pine listens, leans,
                shallow roots lifting and

lowering like a pot's lid riding a rolling
                boil, confirming his prediction

as accurate. My neighbor lost three
                during the last forecast,

had their resinous remains chain sawed
                and discarded, leaving tidy piles

of sawdust in a sad row of open slots.
                But today, while observing this new

weather front, I have an unobstructed view
                of a snow swept mountain, pearlescent

beneath a cracked canopy of cloud—some wonder
                inherited from the three vacant spaces,

which got me thinking back to last winter,
  hiking a dense forest, how I marveled

at a long stalk of light felled across
  a mountain stream, a gift passed down

by an empty lot of a tree. I was a child
  when my mother died. Decades

later, I discovered her gift
  growing in the fallow field of me.

Blame It on Maine

walking to breakfast
the smell of beach rose and pine
his hand brushes mine

Midlife Nightlife

They weren't bad for a tribute band
                    or for an after dinner after thought,
but to be totally transparent, it took peeping
                    through the front doors, past the grand hall
and onto the battleship gray stage (with its illumed
                    backdrop of a harvest moon) to lure me
to the sly ways of the ticket master, the gravity
                    of his grin from behind a double-Dutch door
(but isn't that always the case with the magnetic
                    moon and his publicist). We claimed two folding
chairs in the narrow balcony of the aging
                    clapboard building, where the woman to my right
mouthed every word to "Happy," while her reading glasses
                    swayed from a crystal chain, each bead a micro
disco ball, casting rainbow prisms along our
                    entire row. He was no Mick Jagger, but
I appreciated his confidence, the way he slid
                    his body along the length of the mic stand,
held onto his beltloops as he traversed the stage
                    in a stutter of a strut, tore off his black shirt,
exposing another black shirt, clingy with a bullseye
                    of a sweat stain worthy of his tribute. But it was
the audience who buoyed me most, the sideline
                    swayers, fist-pumpers, and freestyle rockers,

suspending,

for the next three hours, the stiff knee, an arthritic
hip, the rusty mind's anchor and its insistence to sit
this one out. We left early, crossed the road to the
old porch of our Inn, where we watched
the patrons zigzag out to their cars or walk back
to town, waxing and waning down the dampened stone
walkway in the amber glow of shop windows,
their singing ebbing in their flickering wake.

King Street

You are my King Street, the mist as it lifts
from the rain's train. You are the gallery we shelter

in from the sun. Yet you are not the art
mounted to its crisp white walls, the painting,

Girl with the Cup of Tea, for she is me. But you are
the thick plaster to which she affixes herself

and the warm light she bathes in. You are the coffee
I sip in the small dark room rich with wood panels,

paintings of britches and boots, hunters and hounds,
and the unfortunate fox looking back over her tail.

I am the unfortunate fox. I know injustice. You are
the justice. But I am also the swizzle stick thick with rock

candy, the answer to your earthiness as I stir. You are the bar,
Amen Street, the fiery glow on cobblestone roads, hoofbeats,

and rickshaws. I am the only female driver of rickshaws.
You are the hand on my back, catch and release. You are also

the mojito, the lime, the rum, and the ice. I am the muddled
mint and trails of moisture tearing down the tall glass.

You are the napkin soaking up the condensation
of the history of me, but more than that, you are the liberation

of me, the freeing, the possibility of me. You are not the window
of which to watch out. You are more—you are the door.

Sea Glass

a partnership of woman

and water—salt and grit—

a salvation salvaged from

another's plunder: sunken /

desperate drifters / battered /

broken / hardly held

together / raked over /

shrunken / sand-blasted /

scraped / cut / worn /

weathered / washed-up /

somewhat salty—but renewed—

a resurrection in frosted

cobalt blue—edges sleek—

little beached wings of glass

Window vs. Barnacle Billy's Live Webcam

Once mountain, my peak went missing
in a puffed-up couplet of clouds.

But now my eyes favor forward—

my screen a sleepy scene of quaint cove and
footbridge, boats parked like periods at the end
of simple sentences. I become gull, and dock,
and slipknot until the sprocket sun stumbles out
of its morning fog, and light, like a million silver
minnows, flickers the rippled surface as the tide
writes itself closer and closer to shore, delirious
with continuous commas, adding *This,* and
This, and *This*—and then I become—*This.*

About the Author

Susan Dines is a poet, children's book author, and recent MFA graduate from the Bennington Writing Seminars. Her poems have appeared or are forthcoming in *North Dakota Quarterly, Kestrel, Slab, Smoky Blue Literary and Arts Magazine, Comstock Review,* and elsewhere. She has been awarded scholarships from the Bennington Writing Seminars and the Bread Loaf Environmental Writers' Conference. Dines's writing was chosen as the 2023 University of Iowa Hawkeye Haiku contest winner, shortlisted for the Fish Poetry Prize, and placed third in both the 2021 Tucson Festival of Books Literary Awards and 2025 Hippocrates Prize for Poetry and Medicine. *Late Arrival* is her debut poetry collection.

www.ingramcontent.com/pod-product-compliance
Lightning Source LLC
Chambersburg PA
CBHW031204160426
43193CB00008B/497
9781639808489